LEARNING IN LOCKDOWN

LEARNING IN LOCKDOWN

*A parent's guide to helping young
children thrive during campus closure*

DYLAN MEIKLE

WITH FEATURED CONTRIBUTOR

Kate Meikle

All rights reserved. No part of this book may be reproduced or used in any manner without written permission of the copyright owner except for the use of quotations in a book review.

First edition December 2020

Illustrations by Karl Speller
Cover design by Sai Pulido

ISBN 978-0-578-81540-4 (paperback)
ISBN 978-0-578-81541-1 (ebook)

Published by Macquarie Publishing Pty Ltd, Canberra, Australia

*To Audrey, Fraser, Maddison and Lucy.
We are lucky to be your parents, in lockdown and forever.*

TABLE OF CONTENTS

Key terms 1

Preface 3

Whatever your reaction to school closure, it is correct 7

Talking to your children about what's going on 21

Getting started: What does the school want from me, exactly? ... 27

Is distance learning getting you down? 33

Routines combat uncertainty 45

Reality check: Give yourself permission for home learning to be just OK 51

Motivating your child at home 57

Fostering a positive home learning environment 67

Practising self care 75

Reframing this experience to find your silver lining 77

Even when the world stops, parenting doesn't 85

Key resources 87

About the author and contributor 91

KEY TERMS

SCHOOL CLOSURE
　When school is placed on pause: the school campus is closed and the educational programme is shut down; no home learning is offered and there is a break in your child's education.

CAMPUS CLOSURE
　Physical school buildings are closed, with educational programmes and learning performed off-site via online platforms.

DISTANCE, ONLINE, AND REMOTE LEARNING
　During campus closure, learning continues through distance, remote, or online learning. Without physical access to the school campus, teachers and students must continue schooling online; also known as home-based learning and e-learning. Modifications to curriculum, lessons, and teaching practices are necessary to shift from in-person to remote learning. This book uses these terms interchangeably.

HOME-SCHOOLING
　The act of parents educating their children at home. Home-schooling is a form of education legally available in some

locations, globally, that parents can elect to perform, and is not necessarily the result of changes to education caused by the pandemic.

Elementary school and primary school

These two terms, elementary and primary, are generally used interchangeably – formalized schooling for young children from Kindergarten through the first six to eight grades.

PREFACE

As the impact and seriousness of the COVID-19 outbreak became progressively apparent during the week of Chinese New Year in January 2020, news spread of the first school closures in China, Vietnam, and Mongolia. Other countries quickly followed with localized or system-wide closures in what has become the biggest global disruption to education since the Second World War. Millions of students have been affected.

Social distancing was an immediate and widespread response to the outbreak, and as the disease raced across the globe, schools closed and communities shut down services and businesses. The importance of slowing community transmission to maintain public health and 'flatten the curve' (the rate of community infection) was a stated priority of many local and national government responses. During this critical time period, a rapid transition occurred in schools from in-person learning and teaching to online platforms where remote learning—without physical contact between student and teacher—became the new paradigm.

Given the nature of the virus, which at a population level has roiled through communities in waves and outbreak spikes, it is anticipated that school and campus closures will continue globally for some time.

Countries or districts may reopen schools and need to rapidly close again, as they respond to additional outbreaks. Other educational authorities may adopt a cautious approach to reopening and will maintain home-based learning for a period that could push parents beyond what they might have otherwise have considered reasonable under any other circumstance.

In many parts of the world, school or campus closure is something that, if it occurs, is usually short-lived and somewhat predictable. For example, although snow days (whereby a school is closed for a day or so after heavy snow due to risks in safely transporting students to school) occur in some places, we are reasonably certain about those months of the year when snow days are likely to transpire. Communities are ready and able to deal with these disruptions, and school districts have their communication channels in place and contingency plans well-rehearsed. Businesses with working parent employees typically understand and cater for these disruptions, as it is an accepted part of the yearly cycle of normal community life. Other types of school closures, say, for a major event (such as the Olympic Games being held in your city), are infrequent, typically well-planned, and offer families lots of prior warning.

Such short-term disruptions due to weather or a major event are incomparable to what we are living through now. The uncertainty, the stress, the risk of infection and illness, and the social isolation associated with COVID-19 lockdowns are contributing to mounting pressure on the mental and emotional health of our communities and families.

And yet, school closure and the disruption it entails can also offer us moments of triumph. From all over the world we have heard tales of resilience, adaptation, and success. We hear of families flourishing together in their home environment. And we read about children who prove to be even better students at home than they are in a classroom setting.

This handbook was written to provide reassurance and validation for the skills you have deployed, and your level of accomplishment, as you support your children at home, and offers additional insights and perspectives, advice and actionable tips to set you, your children, and your family up for success.

This handbook is for parents coping with the major life disruption of a school closure. It contains the contributions and observations of working parents and education professionals who have lived through their own campus closure with young children, and who have helped support their community through it. In this handbook you will find not only sound advice, based on first-hand experience, but also advocacy *for you*, because your family can't make it without you.

After all, even if the world is crazy right now, your family doesn't have to be.

WHATEVER YOUR REACTION TO SCHOOL CLOSURE, IT IS CORRECT

OUR INDIVIDUAL REACTIONS to the COVID-19 pandemic, and the social and economic fallout associated with it, are as varied and unpredictable as the virus itself.

You probably remember when you first heard about COVID-19, and when it impacted your locality. As the world woke up to the severity of the pandemic, people everywhere wondered what they should do next. Whether it was planning how to keep their family safe, stocking up on supplies, or considering multiple contingencies for travel arrangements, everyone wanted to do what they could to safeguard their families.

On top of all this, the sudden changes the coronavirus outbreak have brought to parents of young children have sent shockwaves through family systems. The closing of schools—and other parts of our community—has forced many parents to make dramatic and responsive recalibrations. Despite all the other roles, responsibilities, and activities that comprise our lives, having to rapidly shift into the added role of home teacher or schoolwork supervisor understandably caught many parents off-guard.

Parental reactions to campus closure have been varied. Some were able to lean into the challenge, and discovered they actually like teaching and having their children learn at home. They find it reassuring to have their children close by, and understand their children's curiosities and academic strengths in a more profound way.

Some parents have found it overwhelming. When our cups were already brimming with the challenges of daily life—keeping our homes clean, our children fed, and our employers happy—how could we possibly add the extra—and unquestionably significant—challenge of teaching our children on top of all of that? After all, our children are too young to learn independently for long periods of time; many are still emerging as readers and cannot process instructions without adult support, and we cannot expect them to navigate the internet to find their teacher's lessons without our consistent supervision and direct help.

Perhaps you fall somewhere in the middle. Many parents I have worked with have experienced a blend of these two reactions. A balanced reaction may acknowledge the positives, but also deeply feel the impact that the challenges of lockdown bring. So, whilst more time spent as a family at home sounds great at the outset, it brings a range of other factors into play, which raises stress levels not just for adults but kids as well. Once the reality of schooling at home kicks in, parents may find this new reality less than appealing, and perhaps wonder how sustainable the situation is. Whilst there is good in the situation, and we may be grateful that we are safe, we also appreciate how unreal and unsatisfactory everything is becoming.

YOU ARE NOT ALONE

IF YOU ARE struggling to get your family through their online learning, you are not alone. If you find it tiresome to navigate the expectations of your child's school or teacher, there are legitimate reasons why leading learning at home isn't all smooth sailing. Remote learning can get 'lost in translation' between school and home—and it likely isn't solely your fault. If you are frustrated by the state of affairs and perhaps notice yourself reacting to things with a shorter fuse than usual, this has become more and more common in homes and families across the globe.

Instead, tune into your reaction to campus closure, and trust yourself. Embrace your feelings. And keep reading this handbook to help you process your feelings and find salient solutions that will help boost yourself and your children.

REFLECTION:

DURING THIS TIME of great change, your reaction may vary, perhaps swinging from enthusiastic to-do-list making to a more sombre reflection on the outcomes for yourself and your children.

- How have you noticed yourself responding to the news of your child's school closing?
- Thinking only about yourself for a moment, can you name all the roles that you are juggling right now? Mother/father, teacher to your child, employee, spouse, daughter/son...
- When you consider all of your facets, where are the

> pressure points? What new challenges have surfaced since school closure?
>
> - What resources do you have, and what sources of support can you draw upon, to help you remain on top of those pressure points?
>
> - What are three tangible things you can do for yourself this week that will promote your own feelings of calm, self care, and wellness?

REACH OUT FOR SUPPORT

IT IS IMPORTANT to identify the sources of support available to you, whether in your localised community or through online communities of like-minded parents. During a pandemic you may find you have just as much in common with parents facing school closure in another country as you do with the parents down the block.

Acknowledge and discuss your feelings about your situation with loved ones or other trusted members of your community; other parents, clergy, or your child's teachers, can help you get through. Counsellors and school psychologists are trained and equipped to deal with stressful situations like this.

In challenging times the support and strength we find in our communities is invaluable, and we must permit ourselves to rely on and trust others, as need be.

NAME THE FEAR TO TAME THE FEAR

AS THE EMERGING reality of school closure sets in, and the school community accepts that, yes, campus is shut and your children are at home, some of your underlying fears and worries may emerge.

For parents already concerned about their child's academic skills or social and emotional development, closing school can invoke feelings of dread. All young children are on a learning journey, and the best place for them to be, obviously, is in school. The school setting, with its trained professionals, ample resources, and structured environment, is designed to deliver hours of quality instruction and learning opportunities each day. Many parents have trouble conceiving of how to replicate or emulate at home all that school provides for their child.

Take a moment to reflect on the hopes and dreams you hold for your child, and also any fears you may harbour. Almost every parent asked could name a fear (or even five) they hold concerning their child's school participation and achievement. We must draw these fears out from under whatever damp rock they are hiding and into the light of reason to examine them, because they are frequently the source of conscious and sometimes subconscious stress.

When we co-exist with unnamed and undiscussed fears for our children's future, we are far more likely to start (over)reacting to the challenges that campus closure presents us with, and small problems become big problems. A Wi-Fi outage becomes a catastrophe! A missed online Zoom lesson becomes the crime of the decade! Our reactions to small problems like these can become overblown, because we are hyped up on the fear and stress we harbour inside, all of which is compounded by the current global pandemic.

Let's look at some of the named fears and worried questions raised when working and talking with parents:

- 'My child will fall behind in school.'
- 'My child already struggles to make friends, and now they are home with me in lockdown and can't see anyone past a screen.'
- 'I don't know how to teach my child to read! The teacher is the one trained to do this! How will my child make any progress?'
- 'My child needs to move and run throughout the day to concentrate. How can they do that at home?'
- 'This school year is wasted/lost. I feel like they were already behind their classmates when all this started. My child's future is affected, for sure.'

So many parents, as part of their love for their child, worry about their child's progress and future. This is normal, and until the pandemic hit, the average parent among us probably kept their fears reasonably in check. But now, under the pressure of campus closure, you may have noticed that anxieties about your children, and how they are progressing and developing, have leapt to the forefront of your mind. After all, in a normal school year, parents inevitably find things to be worried about—but during school and campus closure? It's like pouring gasoline on a fire.

With our children, the stakes are always high, which is natural, because we care so much about them and our performance as parents. How much pressure we place on our children—and on ourselves, as parents—varies from family to family, but it is always there, to some degree.

REFLECTION:

MAKE THIS REFLECTION more concrete by considering writing your responses down on paper or taking a note in your phone.

- Can you name a fear you hold for your child?
- Can you discuss your fear with a partner, another parent or perhaps your child's teacher? If so, what do they say (or what do you imagine them saying) about your fear?- Is the size of your worry congruent with what these trusted outside sources might say about it? Has your fear become overgrown when compared to what other voices of reason in your life might observe?
- What additional information do you need to understand the content of your fear? For example, if you are worried about your child's reading, what do you know about the age range in which children start to read? Are your fears based on reasonable assumptions?
- Let's face it: a school closure may not be the right time for you to tackle the concerns you hold for your child's schooling. Would it be possible to circle back to whatever worry you are holding when the world straightens itself out again? Can you park

> your fear to the side for now, and trust that the worst will not eventuate?

SUCCESS FOR YOUR CHILD

W**HEN WE FACE** our worries during school campus closure, we ponder not only the reasonableness of our fears but also how reality matches up with them. When we think about learning at home being the new reality, this raises the question of what success looks like for your child, in a home learning environment. How will you, as your child's advocate, navigate home learning so that your child experiences that success?

The coming pages will ideally enable you to gain greater clarity on what your child's experience could look and feel like as you embark on distance learning together.

> ### REFLECTION:
>
> C**ONSIDER YOUR CHILD**'s physical, emotional, and academic profiles. Include what you know about your child as a young learner from past school reports and teacher/parent conferences.
>
> - Knowing your child as you do, what are the strengths and challenges they face?

- What does a reasonable picture of success look like for your child? Can you visualize what might success look like for your child in your home learning environment? Can you write this down in a sentence or two?

CHANGES IN THE LEARNING ENVIRONMENT HAVE IMPACTED LEARNERS AND FAMILIES

LET'S BE HONEST: learning at home is not the same as learning at school, no matter what good intentions our education systems or politicians may have. Differences between learning in person at school and via technology at home are vast, and these differences impact each student in different ways. Whilst some children can get along at home in much the same way as they do at school, we also know some children do well at home, while others find distance learning a huge challenge.

Take, for example, a learner whose strength in school is comprehending and processing information when listening. The shift to online learning may have tipped the focus of instruction heavily towards reading, which presents an area of challenge for many students.

Other learners might find it difficult to muster the required level of self-management skills to get their distance learning completed without immediate access to their teachers for scaffolding and support.

And so, we find ourselves in a situation that exposes learning vulnerabilities, and academic strengths that your child relied on in the classroom may not be available to them to draw upon.

We have seen that, during campus closure, a parent's fears are maximised, normal school teaching and learning has been thrown out the window, and, on top of it all, your child is being asked to learn in ways that may or may not enable them to succeed.

ADVOCATE, BECAUSE EVERY CHILD IS UNIQUE

TEACHERS KNOW THAT everyone learns differently, and it is their job to differentiate their instruction to cater to all the children in their class. Differentiation is 'teacher talk' for how educators tailor lessons and learn to maximize the potential success of each child.

When we start by understanding that each child has their own strengths and challenges, and that each child in a class is at a different point of development in their learning, it becomes evident that a given lesson won't work for every child in every class. Variance among learners is normal and commonplace in every classroom. As such, teachers are expected to consider their learners when they prepare lessons, and should offer tasks that contain multiple avenues to success.

In a flexible and well-run classroom, the teacher may offer students different tools to promote individual and whole class success, such as different amounts of time for a learner to complete work, different grouping strategies, different choices within a task (e.g., the teacher gives the class topic options in a writing task), or different materials or ways of demonstrating the same learning.

The takeaway from this is that your child is unique, while often the schoolwork provided during distance learning is uniform. And this is where (after reflecting on the questions about your child as an individual learner, above), as a parent, you can provide your child's teacher with information on what works and what doesn't work for your child. And you can, as need be, step in to manage the times where there is a mismatch between expectations from your child's school and the reality in your home. What your child's teacher may not know is how their student's subjective experiences of learning from home have challenged or benefited each child—and how this differs from the student they knew so well in the classroom. Being an advocate for your child, your family, and yourself (by saving your sanity), is a reasonable role for you to adopt.

If the work set is too hard for your child, remember, this isn't your child's fault. It is up to the teacher to send differentiated work that is targeted at where your child is in their learning and what they need to learn next. Communicating learning issues to your child's teacher should be something you are comfortable doing, and the school should be able to respond with adaptations to make the work they provide both motivating and the right-sized challenge for your child to tackle.

Parents who have had to shift into the role of schoolwork supervisor may have uncovered many new insights about themselves and their children, some gratifying and exciting, others less so. Whatever your reaction to school closure, whether you are gung-ho and ready to take the leap into home-schooling, or you have encountered significant challenges, it is important to know that your reaction is correct. Trust yourself. How you feel, and the advocacy you can provide for your child, is unique to your experience, and your reaction is 100% correct for your context. Don't fall into the trap of comparing yourself with any other parent or online parenting guru. Start with where you are, start with who your children are and what they need as learners, open communication channels with your child's teacher, and go from there.

❝❞
A PARENT'S PERSPECTIVE: INSIGHTS FROM A MOTHER WHO HAS BEEN THERE

I've been shocked, angry, frightened, and stressed since school closed. I've been dealing with enormous changes in my work, and all the while trying hard to be a 'good' mum to our kids.

Married, with two kids aged six and four years old, this year is their first experience of school and preschool, I have been concerned that their first steps into schooling have been negatively impacted. What do my husband and I know about how to teach a six-year-old to read? How can I play 'teacher' and get their attention and focus, like their highly trained real teachers can?

We are all playing our parts, trying our best, and I know that my children need me more than ever, but I mourn my lack of freedom, my decreased ability to work, and a change in my identity after long days at home with the children, with the added cleaning that comes with having everyone home all the time.

Families we know are all negotiating, doing the maths and working out how this new normal is going to be, uncertain of when the kids can go back to school. Who will stay at home? Who will 'work'? Who still has a paid job, and how will we divide the increased home duties and parenting?

Home schooling will test us all, but the ability to set young learners up with their tasks and support them when they cannot read very well, at the same time managing younger children or babies, will be very hard for me. I feel overwhelmed!

My daughter decided to start giving herself a new hairstyle (think mohawk) with a pair of safety scissors last week. Total parenting fail! But I promise I wasn't taking a work call at the time!

It's a full-time job and parenting was never meant to be done in isolation.

—Kate

TALKING TO YOUR CHILDREN ABOUT
WHAT'S GOING ON

Discerning adults keep themselves updated on coronavirus outbreaks from reliable sources, but children and teenagers may not be able to filter useful information for their immediate context, or differentiate between credible and inaccurate sources. If you or members of your family are receiving the bulk of your information from social media platforms, these are notorious for rampant speculation. Unfounded conspiracy theories spread quickly on social media sites like Facebook, YouTube and TikTok.

At a local level, your immediate school closure and the situation unfolding in your community can result in misinformation being spread on Facebook or chat groups. Vet any information you receive before you act on it by cross-checking with your local government or school's website. Rumours can move quickly through communities, especially rumours about the ending or extension of social distancing restrictions. Before you pass on what might be nothing more than a rumour, pause and consider what your motivation to do so might be, and whether there might be any unintended negative effects if the rumour is untrue. In one instance, after three weeks of school closure, a rumour spread like wildfire that schools would reopen on the coming Monday. This generated a rollercoaster ride of emotion (and eventual disappointment, when schools didn't reopen) for many parents who had believed it without verifying it first.

As for young children, who are not developmentally ready to digest news articles with full understanding, it is doubly important for parents to help their children understand what is going on. By now, your child has been through the basic stages of exposure to coronavirus information and should be well versed, for example, on the importance of frequently washing their hands. Changes such as school closure can offer you a window to retrace these conversational steps with your child, and to check what they know and understand. They may hold misconceptions that are worth uncovering and correcting.

Talk to your children using age-appropriate language about the virus, because understanding the infection will reduce their anxiety. Take special care to monitor your own levels of stress and the verbal and non-verbal aspects of communication you present to your children when explaining that their school is now closed. After all, if you were talking to a counsellor about a major issue and they were flailing about, sitting uncomfortably in their seat, and raising their voice in angst, you wouldn't find the conversation very comforting. You must offer a calm version of yourself if you want your child to take their cues from you and not overreact. Remember: children pick up on adults' worries, whether expressed orally or through body language.

And don't forget, if you botch the presentation or the content you convey to your children—perhaps with tears or emotion creeping into your eyes or voice—it is OK to simply sleep on it and try again tomorrow. Children benefit from circling back to topics, as this deepens their understanding.

Children may ask questions we cannot answer. It is perfectly acceptable for adults to say, 'I don't know, but doctors and researchers from all over the world are trying to find the answers'. Tell your child they are safe, and teach and remind them to follow the published guidelines for staying healthy.

Distressingly, COVID-19 has and is causing fatalities internationally. When children hear references to death, whether by watching TV news or hearing adults discuss it, they can become worried and anxious. Consider the age of your child, and their preparedness to understand and cope with troubling news images before broadcasting them via the television or other electronic devices in the public areas of your home. You may not think that children are listening or watching, but so often they soak up far more than we might expect.

Depending on the age of your child, they may not understand why school is closed and they are now learning at home. For example, a young child may not know what a virus (any virus) is, and how it spreads. You may need to build age-appropriate knowledge to increase understanding and reduce anxiety. More and more age-appropriate materials are being commercially produced to help you with this. The free ebook with illustrations by *The Gruffalo's* Axel Scheffler is, in my opinion, a particularly good choice. (You can find the link in the Key Resources section at the end of the book.)

When schools close, it is almost always uncertain when they can safely reopen again. It is healthy and correct to acknowledge to your child that maybe 'no one knows' when regular school will resume. Your child will take their cues from your calm and steady approach to the changing situation. Modelling for your child that you are (at least outwardly) comfortable with ambiguity can go a long way towards promoting an untroubled home environment.

HIP TIP: SCRIPT IT OUT

IF YOU FIND yourself confronted by a difficult conversation—perhaps you need to let your child know that someone at school has become unwell, a grandparent is in the hospital, or perhaps they will miss a major life event (like a birthday party that has been cancelled)—it might be wise to write yourself a short script and read it out loud to your child. Now, that might seem a little strange; however, young children may not even notice that you have written your thoughts ahead of time. Counsellors frequently provide teachers with scripts when a school needs a delicate message conveyed. A script reduces the likelihood of teachers improvising or offering unhelpful additions to the message. It also allows the school to be highly intentional about what they say. If you need to break some tough news and you are worried you are too emotional or will get flustered, try the script strategy.

THE IMPACT OF SCHOOL CLOSURE ON KIDS

OUR SCHOOL COMMUNITIES frequently act as a bedrock for the children, parents, and faculty within them. Losing access to school premises, including classrooms, and to friends and beloved teachers is significant. Once our children have transitioned to school, a new aspect of identity is forged that exists outside the identity they hold as a member of your family. Our children always remain our kids, but they also expand their identities to become school children, students, and pupils. Our kids become proud of themselves as young people who are capable school students, and they develop a sense of belonging to their classes. Thus, the change for our young children, when they can suddenly no longer physically attend school, cannot be understated.

GETTING STARTED:
WHAT DOES THE SCHOOL WANT FROM ME, EXACTLY?

Schools communicate in their own industry jargon and, as adults, it is hard enough for us to keep up with the communication coming from schools and teachers, let alone decipher what is going on and what we need to do.

In a world that fires information at us rapidly, it can become confusing and unclear as to which messages we parents need to tune in to. Has it been communicated clearly to you how your child's learning at home will occur, what the teacher's role will be, and what the parents' role will be? Possibly not, or at least not in ways empathetic to your experience as a parent.

When schools close, there is a flurry of activity as the school administration guides the transition from in-person to remote learning. What may be lost is empathy and understanding from schools for the parents of young children, who are left to pick up so much of the responsibility and actual day-by-day work. Too often, schools push out online learning platforms, and rightly feel proud of their hard work, yet fail to ensure there is no disconnect between the school and home environment. Whilst teachers and administrators try to remain professional, the more efficient and corporate schools behave, the more parents can become disengaged, overwhelmed, or disconnected from the success the school seeks. If you feel like the transition to learning at home has been hollow, the reason may be that the school (despite the best of intentions) has missed the mark, having brought untrained parents onboard as the primary educators of their children.

Our young children have no frame of reference for this change and upheaval, except that which you build for them. You need to explicitly explain to your child how they will learn, what it will look like, and how you will help them. Before you can do that, you need a clear understanding of these facets yourself.

Previously, as a parent you might have been on top of your home-school communication, or at least, like many of us, you did your best. Unfortunately, despite everything else that is going on in your life, you need to invest in your home-school communication in the coming weeks like never before. It is vital to figure out what is expected of you by the school, how to navigate the digital channels and applications being used, and how your child's teacher will communicate with you and the frequency of their feedback. Tuning halfway into the communication from the school will only serve to raise your blood pressure, come that fateful Monday morning when it is time to connect your child to their first video conference class. Forewarned is definitely forearmed in this situation.

Your child's school bears real responsibility as well to support families transitioning to home-based learning, and offer quality teaching resources in this new digital environment. This book is written for families with young children, and it is very clear to schools that children in the first years of schooling are not developmentally ready to be independent learners and in charge of their own education. Children need their teachers, and now their teachers need you—the parent/schoolwork manager—more than ever. With that said, your child's school should clearly communicate with you about:

- The technology they expect you to use, and provide you with any needed logins and links. (Once shared, logins and links need to be managed by you and stored for easy retrieval—a note on your phone, pinned to the wall, or stuck on the fridge—whatever works for you.)
- The expectations and the assignments/learning tasks that are set, how to submit them to the teacher, and what types of teacher feedback you can expect about your child's work. Feedback is everything, whether in person or in remote-learning environments. If you notice that your child (and you) are pushing out work but not receiving feedback, comments, and corrections, then something is wrong with the model your school is using. You should not find yourself and your child on a treadmill of busywork, without actually having your child's thinking, creations, and work assessed and valued by the teacher on the other side of the screen.
- What a typical day of learning looks like, and how they plan to structure the week.
- What is a reasonable amount of schoolwork for your child's age and development, and how long should they spend on each task.

HIP TIP: THREE THINGS YOU CAN (INITIALLY) HELP YOUR CHILD WITH:

1. Help structure the day for your child to enable them to be productive and timely in completing schoolwork. Include free time/play, physical activity as possible, and regular food and water breaks, just like a normal school day.

2. Help manage their technology for, or with, them. Whilst parents may assume children are digital natives and can manage technology without help, the reality is that, although a child may demonstrate confidence playing on a favourite app for fun, this doesn't always translate into the self-management skills required to log on to the internet, navigate to a school's website (or similar), and connect to the right link (and at the right time). Even when a child can manage such a complex and multi-step task, the moment one part changes, or something breaks down, it can leave their cognitive wheels spinning. For example, children whose internet connection dropped out have sat in front of their screen waiting for their connection to Zoom to magically re-open, because they didn't know how to problem-solve themselves. A parent shared that their child sat in front of a screen, waiting, for the remainder of their dropped Zoom call: 35 minutes. The student was

stuck, and they didn't have the problem-solving script internalized that would prompt them to independently ask for help from their parents (who were only a call-out away in the next room). It is worth remembering that online learning is new to our kids, and they just don't have enough experience trouble-shooting technical issues to be independent yet.

3. Stay positive, upbeat, and model being a problem-solver (or at least fake it when in front of your child). Use the classroom strategy called 'think aloud' when you are setting up schedules or technology for your child. Think-alouds are useful when your child is sitting with you and you are showing them how to set something up—in this technique you simply talk through all the steps you are taking, explaining aloud what you are doing. It makes your thinking audible.

It might sound something like this:

'Hmm, it's time to connect to the schedule that your teacher sent us. Let's see if I remember how to do that... Ah, here we go. I click on the icon for the internet browser, and I look for the bookmark we made last week for the class website...'

IS DISTANCE LEARNING
GETTING YOU DOWN?

UNLIKE REMOTE WORLD news stories that do not directly touch us, whenever a school is closed (whether COVID-19 cases are present in the immediate community or not), the impact of the coronavirus outbreak is felt in every home.

Distance learning has safeguarded communities; however, it has also disturbed the routines, home lives, and family dynamics of parents whose children cannot attend school on campus.

No matter where you are, or how long you have been enduring remote learning, the stress of your circumstances can affect your wellbeing and your family's interpersonal relationships. Added to this is the challenge for parents to become full-time schoolwork supervisors. Your child, or children, have also needed to adjust to a different role, that of distance learner, and had to see their parents in a new light.

If you and your family are struggling with these new roles, give yourself permission to take a break. Be aware that you might be suffering from a form of culture shock. Step out of the moment you find yourself in and do something different that helps you to reconnect with your family in more familiar ways. As the adult in the situation, you have the unique power to switch your family's gears and turn your steering wheel in a different direction. Whilst there are times when gritting our teeth and persevering is important, if you find yourself overwhelmed with young children in the house, consider redirecting your family towards activities that heal and foster positivity. Every family is different, but taking a spontaneous walk around the block, creating a delicious dessert in the kitchen together, or pulling out a board game to play might just be enough to re-establish normal life for a brief period.

A CULTURE SHOCK MODEL

WHILST THERE ARE different definitions of culture shock, most models present four distinct phases regarded as contributing to the phenomenon known as culture shock. These phases—the honeymoon period, frustration, adjustment, and acceptance—are laid out below, and we make connections between them and the experience of transitioning to a home learning environment. Using a model like this to describe a cycle that many adults commonly go through helps us understand that we share many of the same reactions and emotions as other parents and people around the world—and that it will be OK.

REFLECTION:

- How might the following phases of the culture shock model apply to your context and your family?
- At which stage might you say you find yourself?

- If there are other adults in your home (spouse, parent, partner), what stage do you think they might be at?

THE HONEYMOON PERIOD

THE NAME SAYS it all—everything is new and wonderful in the honeymoon period. Your days start with novelty, energy, and positivity.

As you transition to becoming a schoolwork manager, you may find all the new aspects of the role exciting, and that you have a can-do attitude. You visualise your child/children working diligently, sharing a joyful lunch break filled with laughter, and you receiving positive feedback and praise from your adult friends, relatives, and your child's teacher. Ahhh! If this is where you are right now—then I encourage you to enjoy the ride! Soak it in!

It is also possible that, in the onset of distance learning, you skipped the honeymoon period. Again, if that was your subjective reaction, that's fine too.

Conversely, like a traveller to another country for a short time, if your home-schooling experience is brief, you may never leave the honeymoon phase. Remember this if you find yourself comparing your experience with that of friends or relatives in other school districts who have experienced school closure for only a handful of days—perhaps they stayed in the honeymoon phase, whilst you (unfortunately) moved on. If the honeymoon was the only phase that your peers experienced, then their levels of positivity about remote learning might be driving you to distraction!

FRUSTRATION

AFTER A PERIOD of time we may find ourselves leaving the honeymoon and gaining a more complex perspective of our new reality. When it comes to travelling to or living in another country, the timeframe for switching from honeymoon to frustration might be months. In the confines of your home, however, your transition to frustration may occur within days, or even hours.

Small things begin to grind on our patience, and we may yearn for a return to what we knew and the routines we previously relied upon. Juggling your added roles and responsibilities may cause frustration to grow. Your child may not live up to the rosy image you had in your head of how eager and active they would be as a student at home. You may notice the impact of taking on your child's education on your own life balance, especially if added to any professional responsibilities. Some models of culture shock call this phase 'negotiation', because we negotiate with ourselves between what we want and what we are actually presented with by life, and this internal negotiation can result in strong feelings of loss and anger, or lesser feelings like annoyance, and perhaps even a fair dose of the blues.

Be kind to yourself when you notice you are within the frustration phase of this new reality. The power in reading about a model like this one is that we can acknowledge, according to the model, that everyone experiences the frustration phase. What you need to watch out for is the duration and intensity of the frustration you encounter.

Some adults who become overloaded and frustrated slip towards anger. Being honest about feeling anger in your situation is important, as is channelling your anger into safe and productive places. The weight of emotional and financial burdens, coupled with losing freedoms and opportunity, can overwhelm. Becoming angry about your situation, and openly expressing this anger in a family environment in which you are all 'stuck' together, can have powerfully negative consequences for the mental and emotional health of your children and others in the household.

HIP TIP: SELF-CARE CHECKLIST

IF YOU FEEL like your emotional state isn't helping to move your family forward, consider these five ideas:

- SELF CARE

    Counteract the impact of your emotions by intentionally deploying strategies you know work for you. Some people enjoy discovering a new podcast, listening to a favourite album, laughing at a comedy movie. Others may enjoy a lengthy read of a book, cooking some favourite food for their family, or trying out a guided meditation app. Go with what works for you and carve out time to make it happen. It is far too easy to put others first, but to be your best self you need to also care for yourself.

- STEADY ROUTINES

    The power of routines is discussed further on in this

book, and is notable especially in terms of the emotional and academic success your children can experience when they are in a positive routine. The same may be true for you, and it may be enough to get you through. Building in your regular sleep and wake times, meal times, and ensuring a balance of screen time (especially reducing the time you spend scanning stressful news articles) cannot be overlooked. Remember, campus closure may turn out to be a marathon, and not a sprint, in terms of the endurance you will need. Routines, just like when a marathon runner successfully slips into a running rhythm, can provide you with the consistency you need to flourish.

- CONNECT WITH YOUR SUPPORT NETWORK

This is a time for you to connect with friends and relatives who care about you. Physical isolation can be countered by the savvy use of technology to video call and connect with people who will build you up and help you find your way through the frustration phase.

- BUILD A KIND AND PATIENT WORLD VIEW

One recommendation: When you find yourself frustrated, lower the stakes and give yourself and your family a break from whatever specific demands are pushing you out of your comfort zone. Take a broader perspective, especially if remote learning tasks and deadlines, or frustrations with technology and connecting your child to the internet, are the sources of your anger. Relax! Your child is safe, your child is learning—and it. is. OK.

- REACH OUT FOR PROFESSIONAL HELP

    A quick online search will provide you with the names and numbers of your local COVID-19 helplines and mental health providers. If you think you should reach out, and haven't done so yet, just do it.

ADJUSTMENT

GOOD NEWS! FRUSTRATION doesn't last forever. Welcome to a better place, known as the adjustment phase. Frustrations subside as we gather our resources, learn from our mistakes, and reimagine what our living circumstances will be like. We may notice some silver linings and gain a more positive attitude. We repeat strategies and behaviours that have succeeded, building new routines and family habits that help us get through.

ACCEPTANCE

THE FEELING OF acceptance, where you are now in the groove and coping in the 'new normal' that has emerged, marks the end of your journey through this model of culture shock. Distance learning may not always be easy, but you now can manage yourself and your family to be as successful and well organized as you were before transitioning to home.

BEWARE OF CABIN FEVER

SELF-QUARANTINE IS NO joke.

Wherever we are in the world, many of us are, or will be, under self-quarantine. Be aware of cabin fever syndrome, which is rooted in the feeling of confinement and isolation for an uncertain period.

Some symptoms may include irritability, restlessness, lethargy, impatience, low stress tolerance, lack of concentration, and decreased motivation.

HIP TIP: MITIGATING THE IMPACT OF CABIN FEVER!

HERE ARE STRATEGIES to help you cope with cabin fever:

- Exercise, and take a short walk outside the home whenever possible (following guidelines to prevent exposure to the virus). Access to daylight regulates our body's natural cycle and releases endorphins. Daily exercise is also a proven treatment for stress and low mood. If you have a garden or balcony, try and get outside more than usual.

- Maintain a normal daily routine and healthy eating patterns as much as possible. Routines and familiarity in times of uncertainty provide a sense of safety.

- Avoid relying heavily on screen and tech as mindless

distractions to pass time. Stimulating our minds without technology (via board games, craft, drawing, reading, crossword puzzles) helps us feel productive and reduces feelings of isolation and helplessness.

- Maintain a positive attitude and ruminate on how you have coped with other difficult situations in the past. You will overcome this too.

- Make sure, as the family begins spending a long time together in confined spaces, that everyone gets their alone time. It is healthy to plan and designate 'time out' from one another. Accept that conflict and arguments may occur between siblings, parents and children, and amongst adults—but notice the level of intensity and frequency, and, if needed, make moves to keep the tone and mood of your home as harmonious as possible, given the circumstances.

FIND YOUR TRIBE AND DRAW SUPPORT FROM THEM

YOU MAY ALREADY have a Facebook, WhatsApp, or similar group chat for your child's class or school. You might have previously connected with a couple of other parents in your child's class, either in the current or in past school years. Now is the time to reconnect, especially if they are also facing the same challenge of school closure you are. At the very least, receiving updates and reminders from other parents in a timely and easy-to-access format can be a lifesaver. Exercise caution, however, if members on the chat bring down the tone and optimism of the group; it is OK to maintain your boundaries and not invite hysteria into your currently overburdened life. Sometimes self care is all about the vibes you *don't* let into your life.

Beyond the empathy and understanding that fellow parents can provide is also real support for the academic tasks you and your child face. Other parents are great sounding boards to bounce ideas off. If you are stuck deciphering the teacher's instructions, it might be easier and quicker to ask a fellow parent rather than communicate directly with the teacher. If you ask a question to a parent group chat, it means making yourself vulnerable, which takes a measure of bravery, but, inevitably, there are other parents wondering the same thing who breathe a sigh of relief that you brought their question up to the group.

Sometimes, support in the physical world can come from other parents too. One family we know created a 'learning pod' with a couple of other families. The parents communicated and set up their shared expectations relating to social distancing and how they could reasonably have their children interact without raising the risk of COVID-19 exposure. Then they practiced a 'divide and conquer' approach to school closure. There are many ways to approach sharing the responsibility for teaching your child at home, and many variables will affect how you set things up (like the children's ages, for example); however, you could consider:

- Each family takes a day or two in the week where they are responsible to teach all the children together in their home
- If they live nearby, one family might host a 'learning playdate' in the morning, and another family host it in the afternoon.

These models depend on the context you find yourself in, the instructions from your local government regarding social distancing, and your own best judgement on safety. Perhaps, these examples have sparked your thinking about how, really, no parent should have to go it alone. Dividing home-schooling and sharing responsibility with other parents can help. If you are also a working parent newly trying to work from home, you will undoubtedly relish and find yourself replenished by even just a few hours without the sole responsibility to teach, motivate, feed, and care for your child.

ROUTINES COMBAT UNCERTAINTY

Once schools are closed, timelines for reopening are usually uncertain and often open-ended. Whether you are reading this at the outset of a campus closure, or you are a couple of weeks in, being mindful of the power of routines with young children is vital.

Distance learning represents possibly the biggest disruption to our regular family life and daily routines that many of us have ever faced. Whilst there are positives and benefits to be had from escaping the 9–5 grind for a while, as the new reality sets in, it is important to keep things simple and reinvest in some parenting basics.

Routines are important for most children, because they provide predictability and certainty. When children are clear about what will happen in a given day, and what is expected of them, they can demonstrate competence and mastery. When things change or are constantly up in the air, children can flounder, and meltdowns and dysregulation will surely follow.

REFLECTION:

CONDUCT A LITTLE self-analysis by considering where your family is, and where you might like to be, as you contemplate these three topics.

Using the sliding scale, what is your current vs. desired state (where are you now vs. where would you like to be?)

Bedtime routine:

Unsatisfactory ←——————————→ *Satisfactory*

Productive mornings:

Unsatisfactory ←——————————→ *Satisfactory*

Increasing independence and responsibility:

Unsatisfactory ←——————————→ *Satisfactory*

MAINTAINING BEDTIME ON A SCHOOL NIGHT

IN FAMILIES THAT enter a home-learning environment, it can, and often does, become normal for them to take a slower start to the day. Without the morning school bell to announce the commencement of the school day, there can be less reason to rush to have all family members up and dressed, breakfast eaten, and hair and teeth brushed. As time passes, the daily morning routine may seem similar to that which we fall into during a prolonged summer vacation.

And yet, we know that young children are fresher and readier to learn in the morning. (This is different for adolescents, who prefer a later circadian rhythm.) As families drift from an active and focused morning, it may become harder to find momentum for the day's learning. Families may miss Zoom calls, find it harder to meet their teacher's deadlines, and generally fall into an air of malaise.

- Whilst your child may not need to be 'at school' by a certain time, maintaining limits on waking and morning routines help them stay in a student mindset and also ready them for the day when schools reopen.
- If your child has drifted from a regular sleep/wake pattern, we recommend slowly moving your child's bedtime. If they are staying up later than normal on a school night, try to walk it back towards their regular time. If you shift bedtime by 15–20 minutes a night every two days, will that get your family back to 'normal' by next week?
- There are cultural and family variances regarding sleep and bedtimes; however, the great equalizer is that school starts at the same time for everyone! According to the CDC, the Centers for Disease Control and Prevention, children in the first few years of school need 9–12 hours of sleep. You know your child best, so if you focus on the time they need to awaken for school and walk that time back 9–12 hours, budgeting additional time to eat breakfast and dress, you have your bedtime goal.

SNAP BACK INTO PRODUCTIVE MORNING ROUTINES

COMBINED WITH A renewed attention to bedtimes, having your children start their day with a series of responsibilities will help shake any built-up lethargy out of your home this week.

- Consider writing or drawing a list of daily 'wake up' responsibilities that your child needs to complete… and then… shhh! No nagging. Let them self-manage through the list. Start tomorrow and see if each successive day this week can run smoother than the last. Keep the list short and attainable, and take an easy win or two before adding additional items to the checklist (with lots of praise for the self management skills your child displays).
- A quick online search for 'printable chore cards' will provide you with inspiration for beautifully presented chore cards (and the opportunity to buy creative efforts from other parents). Chore cards can be customized to what you need your children to get done, and the cards offer your children a tangible way to navigate their daily to-do list. Just like in a classroom, giving children a visually appealing deck of cards that can be laid out on a table and sequenced and flipped when the job is done is an excellent way of building your child's independence.
- For working parents, there is a fundamental change in your schedule to consider too. When once you may have dropped your child at school before turning your undivided attention to your own working day, now your professional responsibilities probably commence at the same time as your

child's—and they are right there, in the house, with you!

Many working parents are surprised by the impact that not being able to devote 100% of their attention to their work life has, and neither can they give 100% to their child's school day. The brutal reality of being an employee *and* a teacher *and* a parent means that corners may need to be cut and compromises made. Any diligent employee may experience a great deal of personal stress when they suddenly find themself a) working from home, and b) simultaneously providing care and academic instruction for their child. As such, getting your day started and your children ready to learn with as much breathing room as possible before online appointments start is a wise move.

YOUR CHILD CAN PROGRESSIVELY LEAD MORE ASPECTS OF THEIR LEARNING

IF YOU ARE now entering your third or fourth week of distance learning, your child/children are not novices at this anymore—and neither are you! In a workshop I co-led, parents were asked what their biggest sources of stress and struggle were during remote learning. Many remarked upon just how hard it is for young children to manage their learning without constant check-ins from adults. A predictable schedule for the school day that everyone in the family can follow is one strategy that will help bring a sense of order to your family's day and week.

- In what ways can you expect your child to extend themself this week and take more responsibility for their learning?

- Could they create their own daily schedule and check off when tasks are complete?
- Could they prioritize which learning activities are the most important to complete?
- Could they start independently using a timer to assign time limits on how long they plan to spend on an activity?

REFLECTION:

- How have your family's bedtimes changed during school closure? Are you comfortable with this change, and have you noticed any benefits or challenges?

- How different are your morning routines these days compared to when the school campus is open? Would your family get out the door on time tomorrow (and do it stress-free) if campus was suddenly reopened?

- Think about your child: what responsibilities can you hand over this week, which they wouldn't have been ready for back in week one?

REALITY CHECK: GIVE YOURSELF PERMISSION FOR HOME LEARNING TO BE JUST OK

As parents we strive for excellent learning from our children. We want to be proud of our children's academic and social successes at school. But what does excellent learning look and feel like at home? It should look and feel like your child's best, and 'best' doesn't mean 'perfect'.

What your child and family's best looks like can change, day by day. No matter how your day goes, rest assured, your best will still be good enough.

If you feel friction or upset between you and your child and you find yourself cajoling them into their day's learning, be mindful of this dynamic and step back from the conflict. If your child seems anxious about completing everything, reassure them that their best is good enough. When we are stressed, we can have a low tolerance to minor problems and higher levels of frustration. Model for your children how to choose to stay calm and manage your big emotions.

GOING INSIDE YOUR CHILD'S TEACHER'S MIND

IT IS LIKELY that your child's teacher is living every waking moment with the realization and appreciation that parents might be finding it tough at home. During school closure teachers deeply appreciate the manner with which their communities have diligently read emails, opened links, navigated new apps and technology, and made it all work for their child. As teachers, we couldn't do it without you, and we know it.

Teachers also know the value of routines, and know that when there isn't a school bus to catch, even getting a child out of their pyjamas in a timely manner might be a struggle.

Rest assured that if your child's teacher is a reasonable human, they also:

- Won't judge you on the volume of your child's distance learning output
- Know your child's distance learning is not a reflection on you as a parent
- Are not playing favourites by sending some families more or less work
- Don't expect all work to be finished perfectly every day

SPARE A THOUGHT (IF YOU HAVE A SPARE MOMENT) FOR YOUR CHILD'S TEACHERS

SPARE A THOUGHT, also, for the stress and changing workplace conditions that teachers are enduring. No teacher ever entered the profession thinking, 'I can't wait to teach Kindergarten online!'

Teaching young children in an online format is probably

the hardest professional challenge your child's teacher has ever faced. Teachers who are jumping into teaching in the online environment are being forced to take risks and significantly adjust the ways in which they work. Add to this that their classroom now includes parents, because parents are either right next to their child, helping keep them on track, or within earshot of the lesson. This level of scrutiny from adults is typically unheard of for primary/elementary school teachers, and the introverts among us can find this particularly challenging. After all, when teaching a class of children, a teacher might not mind if they don't have the greatest singing voice (and the class doesn't mind either); however, you can imagine that being forced to karaoke on Zoom to an audience of children *and* parents isn't exactly a thrilling prospect for most educators.

According to edutopia.com, teachers make about 1,500 decisions each day. These decisions, made minute-by-minute as they engage with their classroom of learners, now have to be made without face-to-face interactions. Teachers regularly adjust lessons, and modify the instruction their students need, based on a range of formative assessment techniques, but one of the best ways in which an experienced teacher works is through authentic connection with their class and students.

The best teachers instinctively know when a lesson is falling flat, and make changes on the spot. Students' body language, energy, and facial expressions signal to skilled teachers when an individual student needs extra help or additional explanation. Yet, these intuitive cues are now lost to us when using online platforms, and teachers report that their zest for teaching has dissipated along with them.

A PARENT'S PERSPECTIVE: KEEPING UP WITH THE JONESES DURING SCHOOL CLOSURE

Amongst the stress and mixed emotions of lockdown, I have noticed how focussed I have been on becoming the 'perfect' distance learning mum. I know deep down that it's a fruitless, anxious exercise, as I am nowhere near perfect!

When other mums posted on our school Facebook group what they had been doing with their kindergarteners, what lessons they did, and extra, creative activities such as baking, gardening, and online yoga, I felt so inadequate. I can't help but compare, and am trying not to get competitive, but some people seem to have adapted better, I suppose, or enjoy being at home more than I do.

Sometimes I half wished that I 'only' had one child to support, as surely it would be so much easier to focus on one child! But when I spoke to my friend who has one child, she says she is worried that her son hasn't had any physical contact with another child since lockdown, which is heart-breaking for him. I realised that every family is dealing with the impacts of school closure in their own way.

Just getting my son to sit with me and read a book has been a big enough battle. Not to mention how my youngest child non-stop interrupts us! It's not her fault—she thinks she is helping, and doesn't like being left out. The best thing I have found is giving her the same work as my son—she gets her own mini whiteboard and enjoys writing her list of words like her big brother.

We start in the morning, so I have had a morning coffee. I get my son's attention and see what the teacher has sent us to do for the day. I aim to do a couple of activities before giving the kids some time to play outside in the garden or ride their bikes around the block. In the afternoon, we do some more school activities, have free-play, colouring in, some TV time, and read books in the evening.

I know the school sends a lot of activities, and they say they don't expect it to be all done, as they want

> to give us choices as to what we do, but I still stress out that we aren't doing enough and the teacher will judge my efforts as a mum. The last thing I want is for my son to fall behind.
>
> —Kate

MOTIVATING YOUR CHILD
AT HOME

MOTIVATION IS A common topic raised for discussion in communities that are experiencing school closure. So, if you are wondering how you can continue to motivate your child at home—almost everyone else is too!

It is natural that all of us—parents and children –- will have our ups and downs. If your child has hit a down patch, then it might be time for you to consider (or reconsider) the tips below and how they might boost your child's motivation.

Whilst younger students are typically developmentally eager to please their parents and teachers, the length of time in which many schools have already engaged in distance learning is taking a toll on the motivation levels of all learners.

In a normal classroom setting, teachers consider which educational 'levers' they can pull to improve the energy, motivation, and performance of their students. The following section covers connecting how teachers work in the classroom and teaching strategies parents can use at home to leverage quality learning for their child and families.

REFLECT TO MOVE FORWARD

TEACHERS ARE REFLECTIVE practitioners. After teaching a

lesson or a unit, a quality teacher will typically reflect, wondering 'What can I do differently next time to improve student learning?' Good teaching teams and schools build ways for teachers to reflect together.

As parents at home, reflecting on how distance learning is going, and making small and large changes, should be expected and is not a sign of defeat! Children and schools are always changing, so the learning dynamic in your home should be flowing and changing too (within reason). If you are living with a spouse or partner, we encourage you (just like good teaching teams) to reflect on the following ideas together.

MAKE SPACE FOR LEARNING

THERE ARE ENVIRONMENTAL cues that help students recognise that it's time to work. By now, you may have already figured out that (ideally) you should create a special place for your child to do their distance learning. This provides students with some cognitive clarity around the idea that 'when my body is in this space, I'm here to work'.

If you haven't yet set up a designated space for your child to do their desk work—give it a try. And if you have set one up, now might be the time to change it up. Variety, after all, is the spice of life, and this rings true for both the classroom and home learning environment.

Teachers frequently move their desks and tables around their classrooms to spark student interest and refresh their spaces. They also use the strategy of 'regrouping' (where children will work in different groups, in different parts of the classroom) throughout the year. Depending on your home setup, you might be able to move your child's learning space, or bring them into closer proximity with siblings or parents also working from home.

You should get your child enthused too: ask them where they would like to set up their 'new' learning space. Have your child take some pride in the space by adding motivating (but not too distracting) items to their work area, like cool pens and erasers. By now, there are lots of images online of people sharing their home school work spaces, but remember, it's not a competition! You know your child best and you know their levels of distractibility and their need for movement and physical and visual stimulation.

Maintain realistic expectation about the length of time your child needs to be seated and focused. Reflect on yourself as an adult and how you are empowered to 'self regulate' when working by getting up to make a hot drink, use the bathroom, or make a phone call whenever you need to. As adults we often take a minute to distract ourselves (check a text message, think about what's for dinner...) and then we jump back into a work task feeling renewed. Don't expect a child to magically have a longer attention span than you do.

Create a space that sends visual cues that 'I'm here to work, not play', and include school-style elements, like the week's schedule and their class photo, posted up clearly. One clever parent told me they write down the day's learning activities on Post-It Notes, and arrange them on the wall nearest their child's desk. As the child completes each task, they physically move the Post-It from the wall onto a poster that the parent and child decorated, labelled 'I've done it!' in eye-catching colours and script.

PROXIMITY IS A TEACHING STRATEGY THAT WORKS AT HOME TOO

ALL TEACHERS KNOW this trick intuitively, and the best teachers deploy it as an intentional strategy. As the saying might go: 'Keep your friends close, and your distractible student closer'.

If your child is unable to complete a distance learning task independently because their ability to manage their time is still developing or their focus naturally wanders, try positioning your child in closer proximity to you.

In the classroom, teachers will 'preferentially seat' (yes, this sounds like flying in premium class) students so that they are physically close to them. Teachers can then pre-emptively provide support if the student gets stuck and monitor their work output to keep energy and focus up. At home you can achieve this by seating your child in a space with you nearby to provide timely help and positive reinforcement.

An example: In my home, my daughter is far more productive and quicker to complete a task when she sits at the kitchen table with me (while I'm also working), than when she is upstairs in her bedroom (alone). Viva the power of proximity!

CATCH AND RELEASE: NOT JUST FOR FISHING

'CATCH AND RELEASE' is a fishing technique where fish are caught and immediately unhooked and released back into the wild.

When you are monitoring your child's learning at home, you should seek to provide them with opportunities to come to you for help and guidance, then 'release' them to a period of independent work. How long that period is, before you 'catch' them again, is dependent upon their age. This is what happens in classrooms—obviously, teachers don't sit with one child all day. Instead, they cycle through their classroom, connecting with each student, providing help and then moving on.

If you are unsure how long your child can reasonably be expected to work independently, ask your child's teacher.

SCHEDULES AND TARGETS ARE OBVIOUS – BUT OVERLOOK THEM AT YOUR PERIL!

IF POSSIBLE, SIT down with your children at the start of the day and co-create their schedule. Just like in their classrooms, they will know what is happening that day and can provide input into the order that they complete tasks.

Making learning targets visible is important for young children. Although *you* might be kept awake at night thinking about an assignment that is due to your child's teacher at the end of the week, don't make the mistake of believing your child is also actively tracking due dates and deadlines. They just aren't old enough to internalize responsibilities and know how to work towards completing complex tasks over time.

In classrooms, teachers use display boards and whiteboards to write up targets and goals for the day/week, and we can do that at home too. Write projects or major activities down for your child, and display them where they can see them. Your daily schedules should make the connection between the projects that need to be done and the time allocation to do them. Break large tasks down into smaller pieces, and write each part down on a Post-it Note (or similar). As your child completes each part of a project, have them physically move the post-it note from a 'to-do' column to a 'done' column. Take, for example, a classic activity: writing a story. Depending on the age of your child, this activity might include variations on steps that include brainstorming, drafting, revising, publishing (writing it neatly) and illustrating. When you notice your child is stuck with an activity, it may well be because they need the parts of the activity broken down for them. Telling a child to 'go and write a story' is very different from saying 'OK, step one: let's brainstorm some interesting characters and a setting'.

TIME LIMITS ARE FAIR AND MOTIVATING – AND THIS IS HOW 'REAL SCHOOL' WORKS TOO

SETTING REALISTIC TIME limits for working can be key to helping kids stay on task. Class periods in elementary schools are usually 40 or 50 minutes long and children have the ability to self regulate by moving around and getting water when they need to in order to work more effectively. They also have the motivating energy of sitting among their peers.

- For example, with a Grade 2 student: use a timer to set a 15-minute work session and then a 3-minute break (water, jumping jacks, quick chat) and then another 10–15-minute work session, followed by a longer break.

HIP TIP: KNOW WHEN ENOUGH IS ENOUGH

SOMETIMES, WHEN YOUR child is doing well and 'on a roll' with their learning, we might be tempted to push them, and keep pushing them, to work for a longer period of time. This temptation is well-intended, but be careful not to overextend your child and undo all the good progress and positive work that has occurred. After all, when a normal school day ends and a child hasn't finished their work, they still get to go home! In this way, children can sometimes leave school 'on a high' and be eager to come back to school the next day to finish their work. At home, if you keep stretching the learning period into overtime, you are likely to demotivate your child rather than get them excited to come back the next day.

In short: stick to your agreed time limits.

HELP YOUR CHILD WITH THE PROCESS, NOT THE PRODUCT

As THE ADULT in the room, you can use your best judgement about when to help your child with distance learning, and what to help them with.

We recommend, when you are looking at the distance learning information/lessons, that you identify quick ways you can assist your child to get set up with a task and ready to do the learning.

For many children, the hardest part of distance learning is setting up all the requirements for the lesson and managing themselves and their time. Saving your child extra minutes, and potential frustration and errors, by helping 'scaffold' the task at hand might be a technique to deploy from time to time.

For example, if a child needs to work with a template, it might be more efficient for you to draw the template quickly and unleash your child to the actual task (which is where the real learning takes place). In the younger years of education, templates are also known as 'black line masters', learning scaffolds that are easily photocopied by the teacher for distribution to their class. (Or at least this is what happens when school is in session!)

Now that you are learning at home, your child might benefit greatly by having you help organize the paperwork for them. Take for example a story-writing task. Most teachers teach writing with an emphasis on structure, and in a normal classroom they might use templates and black line masters that help their students work through the different sections of a story. At home, by carefully analysing the demands of a task, you can help provide your child these same structures. So, for story writing, you might create a page with three large rectangles—arguably easier if you have a printer at hand—and ask your child to consider the 'beginning', 'middle', and 'end', and assign each to a respective rectangle. For older children you might prompt them with key words like 'setting', 'problem', and 'resolution'.

Helping out in this manner also helps chunk a learning task down into manageable bites, leading to a more motivated child. Follow your child's teacher's lead, and keep an eye out for shortcuts like these that will further engage your child with their learning.

It might help to think of yourself as a member of a Formula 1 car racing pit crew whose job it is to quickly change the racing car's tyres, enabling the driver to get back out on the track without losing too much time. In the same way, as adults, there are quick fixes and structural supports that we can quickly deal with which allow our kids to continue with their learning.

ASKING THE RIGHT QUESTION LEADS TO THINKING AND ACTION

INVITING YOUR CHILD to think for themself, and to approach learning in an open and curious way, is a key component to a normal classroom interaction between a student and teacher. Master teachers become very adept at posing questions that position the student as an active part of the learning process. Teachers typically do not rush to solve a problem for a student without 'tossing the ball back' once or twice and attempting to elicit action from the learner.

Child	*Effective Parent Response*
'I don't know what to do.'	'What *do you* think needs to happen?'
'I don't get it.'	'Can you read me what the question says?'
'This is too hard.'	'What is the *first* part of the activity? What do you need to do *first*?'

FOSTERING A POSITIVE HOME LEARNING ENVIRONMENT

IT MIGHT BE time to reflect on the levels of positivity that you are orchestrating in your home school. Educators know that positive relationships with relaxed and happy students maximise learning outcomes. In this section we invite you to consider how you might give yourself and your child permission to de-stress and come back fresh to learning.

GOOD EDUCATORS *DO NOT* EXPECT YOU TO COMPEL YOUR CHILD TO WORK

EVERY DAY IN classrooms, teachers ask students to be ready to learn and to give learning their best shot. But when children at school are tired, sad, or frustrated, teachers switch gears, because they know children cannot learn when they aren't ready to learn.

Although we might feel pressure to keep our child on task and as productive as possible, your child's teacher would be troubled to learn that students are being held to standards at home that are *higher* than those of the normal classroom.

When in doubt, ask your child's teacher about what success looks like for your child.

KEEP IT UPBEAT AND INVEST IN LEVITY

IN NORMAL CLASSROOMS teachers use rigour, high expectations, *and* humour and empathy in equal measures. Don't underestimate the power of a few jokes and a 'brain break' along the way.

RELEASE THE PRESSURE

IF YOUR CHILD is feeling pressure, ask yourself what the most important outcome is for your child's learning that day. Do you run the risk of winning the battle (pushing your child to finish a particular assignment or task on a given day) while you lose the war (your child will be less and less motivated about distance learning and have a harder time coming back to their learning at home with energy and excitement)?

Whilst teachers encourage, challenge, and sometimes push children in their learning, they also know when a child has had enough. Stressed kids don't learn, so sometimes it is best to call it a day and come back fresh the next day. Never be afraid of 'strategic abandonment' of a task either. Modern education is cyclical in nature insofar that children will typically spiral through cycles of instruction on particular topics. They frequently revisit content in order to deepen understanding over months and years (e.g., no one learns multiplication in one sitting). All this means is that if, on a given day, you feel your child needs to only complete a reasonable amount of work rather than *all* of the set tasks, that's fine! Rest assured that your child will be exposed to similar content and learning activities again, in probably the near future. You can't fall behind from one bad day.

LET GO OF THE ROPE

LETTING GO OF the rope evokes an image of two hounds locked in a never-ending tussle, each pulling on one end of a length of rope. So it can be within our relationship with our children when learning at home.

If you find yourself stuck in a battle with your child for power and control over home learning, don't forget that, as the adult in the scenario, you have the maturity and wisdom to know when it is time to choose to let go of the rope and disengage from the tension and struggle. Remember; you wouldn't want your child at school to be in a learning environment that involves pressure, cajoling and arguments, and nor should it be that way at home. Children enjoy a level of familiarity and security with their parents that they don't have with their teachers. As such, we are certain that, at times, your 'student' is going to push your buttons and treat you in ways that they would never dream of doing to their teachers. For some parents this has been the hardest part of trying to teach their own children. When you find yourself in a tug-of-war with your child about learning, coach yourself into letting go of the rope, then take time for yourself and come back fresh and ready to teach another day.

POSITIVITY AT HOME, JUST LIKE AT SCHOOL

DON'T FORGET TO notice and praise success—and do it early and often. No matter your experiences this week with distance learning, your family will have enjoyed a number of successes. It is up to you to notice and celebrate them!

It could become too easy to fall into a 'glass half empty' approach to distance learning. Yet, honouring and talking about the great things that you and your children have done this week is actually a more satisfying and psychologically healthy approach to take. It may even lift your spirits beyond heavy skies and ongoing troublesome news stories.

HIP TIP: THE POWER OF POSITIVITY!

THERE IS A well-known rule of thumb when it comes to dishing out praise and criticism, and that is to give roughly five positive comments per each critical comment. That seems like a lot, and it might not be happening in your house right now, but why not give it a try? You can run a little scientific experiment and notice if you can extract a change in the atmosphere in your home by running a 5:1 compliment ratio. It's said to work in romantic relationships too, so what do you have to lose?

SCREEN TIME AND THE NEW NORMAL

SOME FAMILIES HAVE noticed that their child, by virtue of the logistics of distance learning, is spending longer periods of time in front of a screen. This may worry you; or perhaps you are ready to accept this as part of the strange times that we live in.

There are different views on how to manage screen time when we are learning at home. Some writers or experts argue that you should throw out the window any reservations about time spent on a screen during home learning, and stress less about it. You can always revert to your regular family agreements on screen time after this is all over.

Because many schools will provide students with instruction online, and perhaps supplement their lessons with app and online games and tasks, you may find that your child is on an electronic device several times per day. If this is the case, then when it comes to free time, perhaps you might like to reconsider whether the iPad or game console is the right avenue for play. For older children we recommend Common Sense Media's (commonsensemedia.org) Family Media Agreements as a solid starting place to discuss with your children and draw up reasonable boundaries on the use of technology.

A PARENT'S PERSPECTIVE: LIVING AND LEARNING BEHIND THE SCREEN

Screen time has always been drummed into us parents as a big issue, and my husband and I have worked hard to set up rules around when and what the kids watch on TV or play games on the iPad.

During a normal school week, we generally allow the children to watch TV after they have had a bath, while I cook dinner. It's a nice wind-down for them and gives me some uninterrupted time in the kitchen. But during lockdown, it feels like the screen time rules and all our routines are out of the window!

My son has to use the iPad for his school work, and then there are the Zoom calls with his class, as well as social calls with friends and family. When I add it up, that's a lot of time staring at the screen that he never would have had.

For a family who has been very conscious and had very set rules about screen time, I worry that we have opened the floodgates… I am already dreading having to reset our screen-time routine when we get out of lockdown. I also find I am using the TV more during the day and letting the kids watch their favourite Netflix shows so I can do some work on my laptop or household chores by myself. Without the TV as the 'digital babysitter', I worry that the kids will get up to all sorts of mischief and quarrel with each other while I am on a work Zoom meeting or need to focus on writing an email.

Yes, I also admit I have bribed my son with a reward of TV if he finishes his school work… not sure the experts would be impressed by this, but sometimes I just feel like 'whatever works' is good enough at this point.

—Kate

PRACTISING
SELF CARE

THE NOTION OF putting on your oxygen mask first, *before you assist others*, was a common message found on aircraft safety guides back when we could still freely access air travel. During forced school or campus closures, the likes of which none of us have experienced before, taking time to practice self-care of ourselves *as individuals* is of the utmost importance. And as we navigate school and campus closures, managing our mental and emotional health *as parents* has never been more vital. Being explicit with yourself about the care that you need is very important. When timelines for schools and communities to reopen are unknown, it is crucial to be intentional about the ways that you can provide yourself with support and resources that de-stress and inoculate you from burnout and distress. Make a plan, write it down, talk about it with your partner or friends to make it real, stick it on the fridge, and take care of yourself.

Taking on the roles of parent, teacher, and adult (all while your own regular life responsibilities continue and aren't suddenly put on hold) may not have been the easiest on you. Consider some rewards for you and your family to put on the calendar (e.g., download a movie the family can watch together; order some delivery food for a special dinner), and focus on how your family, and the learning that you have helped orchestrate, *is actually excellent.* Considering everything going on in the world right now, it's time to give yourself some kudos for everything you have managed these past days and weeks, and perhaps months.

REFRAMING THIS EXPERIENCE TO
FIND YOUR SILVER LINING

IN THESE UNSETTLED times of distance learning, campus closure, and disjointed family routines, our global and local communities have become more resilient through adversity.

> '[S]ome are born great, some achieve greatness, and some have greatness thrust upon 'em.'
>
> —(ACT II, SCENE V, OF SHAKESPEARE'S *TWELFTH NIGHT*, 1602)

Teachers are either working from home or, in some situations, on a campus bereft of children. Our students endure temporary exclusion from their school learning environment, and they surely miss their peers and friends and pine for *direct* contact with their teachers. Parents have continued to manage their new and unexpected roles, in which they are being asked to be everything to everyone. Little wonder that nerves might be frayed and our individual and collective patience is likely to be wearing thin.

AND YET...DOES RESEARCH UNVEIL A SILVER LINING?

THE CHALLENGES THAT our community members have faced, whether they be students, educators, or parents, are not for nothing. The time that you have endured in a home learning environment is not lost to you. Instead, we all have the opportunity to find a broader meaning from these weeks of campus closure.

And if we can find it for ourselves, we can teach and model it for our children.

Reframing is a therapeutic technique that counsellors and psychologists use to encourage a client to look at a situation or experience in a different way. Encouraging ourselves to challenge our perspective of the pandemic and relook at our situation may cause us to notice some hidden benefits or silver linings that were actually there all along.

As a way of reframing this experience, let's take a look at the Human Skills Matrix, out of MIT, the Massachusetts Institute of Technology. The Human Skills Matrix makes for interesting reading in its own right, and is highly compelling as we consider what a set of 'essential non-technical skills' might look like for the day when our children mature into the workforce and seek to professionally 'thrive in today's digitally powered organizations'. This is a research-based, future-looking and up-to-date way of considering the uniquely human skills that our children will need to develop as they grow and mature. (The link to the public website explaining the Human Skills Matrix can be found in the Key Resources section at the end of the book.)

> 'Resilience is a muscle. Flex it enough and it will take less effort to get over the emotional punches each time.'

— Alecia Moore (aka Pink)

If we accept the message in the quote from Pink, and believe that human traits such as *persistence, initiative,* or *empathy* do become stronger the more we access and use them, perhaps we may also see that through the challenge of campus closure, a form of personal growth has been experienced by all.

REFLECTION:

- What do you notice about how campus closure has inadvertently provided you and your children with chances to flex your *persistence, initiative,* and/or *empathy* muscles?
- Consider how our *comfort with ambiguity* levels have been deepened in ways that will benefit us and our children later in life.
- Is it also safe to say that our *adaptability quotient* has increased fourfold during this time?

Often in life, it is the challenges that we face that help refine our character and define who we are. Although campus closure may have forced us to live and learn in different ways, it is through challenges like this that we grow and become actualised adults.

The Human Skills Matrix is just one way of reframing this unique period of time in a more positive light, and you may have already discovered your own silver lining through other resources or your friendships, faith, personal philosophies, and/or families.

We all wish for robust character development for our children, students, and, indeed, ourselves. Perhaps through these weeks and months of COVID-19 upheaval, the foundation of greatness, in many small and large ways, has been thrust upon us all.

A PARENT'S GUIDE

> ##
>
> ## A PARENT'S PERSPECTIVE:
> ## LET'S HEAR IT FOR THE KIDS...

Resilience is the buzzword of all the parenting books and blogs, but there's nothing like living through a pandemic to really bring it out in our little people, is there?

Through the difficulty of home-schooling and all the problems that COVID-19 has thrust upon us, when you bend down and look at it from a child's perspective, their world has duck dived, been pulled apart and back again, and yet they have mostly coped remarkably.

They repeatedly hear the words 'because of the

virus...' Dot, dot, dot - the dots have ranged from disappointments that are hard to rationalise to acutely painful and upsetting news:

'Because of the virus, we can't go to play in the park, ...see friends, ...hug anyone, ...go to the shops, ...go anywhere.'

Even as restrictions ease, there is still a daily share of disappointments for kids and implications to what they look forward to and expect will happen in their lives, because that is the way it's always been for them.

Because of the virus, we can't walk into school to drop you off.

Because of the virus, you can't visit your family interstate.

Because of the virus, Mummy can't volunteer in the classroom and help the Kindy students learn to read, or watch your Book Week dress-up parade at the school.

Because of the virus, no mucking around at the shopping centre, and you must stay away from people.

Because of the virus, your cousins won't be coming for Christmas this year. Ouch, that one hurts a lot.

They say that the way we have dealt emotionally with the pandemic is similar to the stages of grief, which includes denial, anger, bargaining, depression, and that gold-star stage of acceptance. (Has anyone reached that yet?)

While I admit to having felt all of these emotions this year, these days I find that bargaining seems to visit me most often, and mainly when it comes to the kids. I hear myself saying things such as, 'So long as the kids can still do most of the things they usually do, so long as they can still have play dates, still go to school, still enjoy birthday parties and playgrounds…, I'd trade that for dot, dot, dot'.

I know there's no way I can bargain my way out of this reality, but I can't seem to help it when it comes to the children. We want our kids to get through this time as safely and happily as they can. We want to shield them from as much of the disappointment this year has thrown at us as possible.

Thankfully, their little tanks of resilience aren't emptied out just yet.

—Kate

EVEN WHEN THE WORLD STOPS, PARENTING DOESN'T

So, how are you doing?

Burnt out? Yes, some of us are.

Tired? Certainly.

Stressed out? Uh, that's going to be a 'yes' again.

You may reach the weekend, or even a school holiday where the home learning stops—except parenting doesn't stop, and while school may pause for a week or a weekend, our parenting continues. For working parents, for single parents, for all parents, each day is a continuation of a stressful, difficult, and unprecedented time in our lives.

It is hard to contemplate how many of us, within our diverse communities, are increasingly worried and anxious for our loved ones throughout the world. Worried for our children. Worried for ourselves. We will each have our stories to tell when these days are done, and we can hope that they are stories of resilience, strength, and success in the face of the impact of this historical event.

As parents, we can already make a claim to the title of 'Distance Learning Veteran'. If that sounds impressive, that's because it is.

We may even be ready to feel proud of how far we have come as parents and as a community.

Our students' levels of resilience, humour, acceptance, and flexibility have been an example to us all.

Our teachers adroitly pivoted to working without direct contact with their students. They have embarked on a distance learning programme that none of them signed up for when they studied to be teachers.

But it is our parents—you all—it is what you have done to hold your families together during this time;

The cooking, cleaning, uploading, cancelling of vacations, arranging online video calls, consoling, cajoling, planning, re-planning, sharing computers, wiping away tears, washing hands, keeping informed, connecting with loved ones... and, through it all, staying hopeful and positive for your children and families.

And we know you will find the strength and courage to keep doing all this and more for as long as your school is closed.

If we could send you all flowers, wine, chocolate—or maybe just give you five minutes to yourselves—we would.

As it is, we send our heartfelt respect.

KEY RESOURCES

THE COVID-19 PERIOD has brought rapid changes and a heightened sense of worry as additional places in the world have become more directly impacted by the coronavirus.

The experience of seeing other places in the world become 'hotspots', and our loved and dear ones become vulnerable, has not been pleasant.

The following resources are not just interesting and topical; they are also reputable resources worth saving for parenting questions and wonderings that go beyond our current world crisis. We recommend bookmarking these sites, or joining their mailing lists.

THE CHILD MIND INSTITUTE

www.childmind.org

The Child Mind Institute is an independent, national non-profit that provides quality resources for parents, teachers, and professionals. Their site is full of specific articles that demythologise common childhood social and emotional issues, as well as guide parents with research-based updates and advice.

POSITIVE PSYCHOLOGY

www.positivepsychology.com

A knowledge base with lots of inspiring and useful articles on the role of psychology in supporting our personal growth. Reading about *resilience* during this period of time will not be time wasted.

SECOND STEP

www.secondstep.org/covid19support

This website compiles lists of resources parents can make use of to consider and teach their child social and emotional skills at home during the challenge of school closure.

HEY SIGMUND

www.heysigmund.com

This website contains news and ideas derived from psychology. Its mission is to provide parents with psychological strategies and insights.

THE GREATER GOOD

www.greatergood.berkeley.edu/

A great one-stop shop for everything related to the science of happiness. Podcasts for parenting, resources for mindfulness, and good readings for getting through life's challenges and coming out a stronger, happier person on the other side.

THE HUMAN SKILLS MATRIX

https://jwel.mit.edu/human-skills-matrix

Referred to in this book by way of a reframing exercise, the Human Skills Matrix offers a research-based framework of the skills predicted to be of value in the dynamism of the future employment market. If we accept, to a greater or lesser degree, that schooling prepares our children for the workplace, this reframing teaches us that the very challenges that campus closure has inflicted upon families have also provided us with opportunities to grow a set of skills that will make us more resilient in the future.

ABC (AUSTRALIA) SPECIAL COVID-19 EPISODE FOR KIDS

https://www.abc.net.au/abckids/shows/play-school/ covid-19/12114308

CORONAVIRUS: A BOOK FOR CHILDREN

https://nosycrow.com/wp-content/uploads/2020/04/ Coronavirus-A-Book-for-Children.pdf

OFFICIAL GUIDANCE:

AT ALL TIMES the authors take guidance from, and adhere to, official advice and communication from reputable government or world health governing bodies. In the instance that the contents of this book vary or differ from official recommendations, please follow the published official advice for your context and location.

We recommend remaining up to date with information from, at the least:

- World Health Organization *https://www.who.int/emergencies/diseases/novel-coronavirus-2019/advice-for-public*
- UNICEF *https://www.unicef.org/coronavirus/covid-19*
- The Centers for Disease Control and Prevention *https://www.cdc.gov/coronavirus/2019-nCoV/index.html*

ABOUT THE AUTHOR AND CONTRIBUTOR

DYLAN MEIKLE, M.ED, B.PSY, B.ED

Dylan is a qualified classroom teacher, school counsellor, educational consultant, and workshop leader. He has experience working with students and their families from pre-Kindergarten through grade five in schools in Australia, China, Vietnam, and Singapore.

He has been previously published on the International Baccalaureate Organisation's (IBO) *Sharing the PYP* blog, and his writing has been included in the IBO's *Primary Years Programme Playlist*, a global resource for parents and teachers. Dylan's writing on innovative classroom design can be found on www.makespace4learning.com, and his work with teachers and schools on this subject has had a global impact. He is an Apple Distinguished Educator (2007).

Dylan lives in Singapore with his wife, two wonderful children, and little brown dog.

@dylan_meikle

KATE MEIKLE

KATE IS A writer, parenting columnist, and director of the Canberra City News. Kate contributed to *Learning in Lockdown's* featured parenting perspectives. She believes in being honest and modelling vulnerability when it comes to writing about the joys and challenges of parenting. She lives in Canberra, Australia, with her husband and two children. Read more from Kate at www.citynews.com.au.

www.ingramcontent.com/pod-product-compliance
Lightning Source LLC
Chambersburg PA
CBHW051407290426
44108CB00015B/2185